ADVANCE PRAISE FROM THE WORLD

Просто смотря на это, ЭТО становится ясным. Читая, то что между слов, этого замечательного произведения искусства, я обнаружил мистический опыт того , насколько все взаимосвязанно, с очень приятным подтверждением через ощущением мурашек по коже.

"I just look at this, and it is clear. Reading what is between the words of this marvelous piece of art, I discovered a mystical experience, how everything is interconnected, with a very pleasant confirmation through the feeling of goose bumps."

Andrey Belyaev

"همانطور که به بسیار عالی نامگذاری شده؛ کتاب "افتادن در همه" ما را به سفری می‌برد که ساختار عقلانی ما در هم گرفتن، ما را به سفری می‌برد که ساختار عقلانی ما در هم شکسته و در حالت تسلیم پذیری و تسلیم قرار می‌گیریم. شکسته و در حالت تسلیم پذیری و تسلیم قرار می‌گیریم. از آن به عنوان منبع الهام برای راهنمای مراقبه روزانه استفاده کنیم."

"As it is perfectly titled *Falling Into All*, this takes us on a journey to collapse the intellectual mind into the beauty of the surrender, by using simple words that have been magnificently arranged one next to another. Great source of inspiration for daily meditation guide."

Raha N.

進入北恩的詩選彷彿左手裡拿著莊子的逍遙遊，右手拿著老子的道德經，清風鳥靜的禪院中徘徊朗詠。
這位詩人多年吸收了各地多方的塵煙，悟覺他各人獨特的文筆，放出他仁慈博愛的歌聲。北恩的歌聲在亂世當頭的目前為我們帶來無限的安寧。

"Entering this collection of Ben's [Bei En 北恩*] poems is, as if one is holding Zhuang Zi's Butterfly Dreams in one hand and the Dao De Jing of Lao Zi in the other in a tranquil Zen garden and hearing their words under a clear breeze. This poet has traversed many traditions and cultures, giving voice to his own words in grace and song. This voice brings comfort, particularly to our world of today."

Tsun Yuan Chen

*北恩 [Bei En] is my transliteration of Ben into Chinese. Literally, it means northern compassion, but it also has an allusion to the contemporary Chinese poet 北島 [Bei Dao].

"He makes the ordinary into the extraordinary, and while he does it, he finds the strength to pause and think it through."

Ingrid Croce
Author, with Jimmy Rock, of
I Got A Name, The Jim Croce Story

"This book is a treasure with each page revealing a door to feel the precious stillness and wonder of being alive. This is no ordinary door, it swings both ways so the reader's inner quiet and wisdom are awakened along with a deep appreciation for the outer. This is definately a book to keep close and read again and again as the messages speak louder with each opening."

Holly Riley
Best Selling Author of *Allowing - A Portrait of Forgiving and Letting Life Love You*

"*Falling Into All* is the perfect salve to soothe your frenzied brain. Ben's poems are beautifully crafted, a juxtaposition of words that have challenged me to let go of the need for structure, answers, next steps, certainty and control, and to move forward instead in wisdom, peace and joy. I dog-eared many pages and marked lines that surprised, moved, and inspired me."

Naomi Fortner

"An inspired distillation of years of meditation on the divine."

Richard Payne

"Das Lesen der Gedichte erzeugt einen Rhythmus, eine Resonanz im eigenen Körper: ein Verlangsamen, dass das Gelesene als körperliche Empfindung geschehen lässt. Ich bin berührt, gerührt! Vielen Dank für diese Erfahrung, mein Freund Ben!"

"Reading your poems formed a rhythm in my body. Everything became slower, and what I read became a body reaction. I'm touched. Thank you, my friend Ben."

 Rosmarie Herzig

"En mans poesi
Låter som hans själs sång,
Uttryckt på så många sätt.
Fastän bara en kommer i åtanke,
Som är i sig självt hjärtat
Jag längtar efter."

"One man's poetry
Sounds like the song of his soul,
Expressed in so many ways.
Yet only One comes to mind,
Being itself the heart
That I adore."

 Bjorn Saw

"Deine Worte sind wie ein guter Freund, der dich an die Hand nimmt und dir zeigt, was wichtig ist."

"Your words are like a good friend who takes you by the hand and shows you what is important."

Jeannette Fischer

"*Falling Into All* exercises the discipline of going inward. The simplicity of verse and economy of word veil deeper meaning, yet Ben manages to launch the reader into a journey to reveal the wisdom of an innate knowing. In our pause he shifts us gently back into a simpler way, with an ease that allows the friendly surrender of the journeying mind. Revealed in these writings is a study of great depth and peace that involves everything and requires nothing but a sincere heart. Beautifully written, it is an enigmatic, profound treatise. Enjoy the journey."

Ginny Breeland

يدمج بن ببلاغة فن الشعر مع عجائب الفلسفة الوجودية
اللامحدودة. كما هو موضوع من منظور فريد ، فإن "ترتيبت الأحداث
التي تمت مواجهتها" يعطي نظرة ثاقبة لاستكشاف المؤلف
للجميع.

"Ben eloquently merges the art of poetry with the infinite wonder of existential philosophy. As described from a unique perspective, an 'arrangement of events encountered' gives insight into the author's exploration of all."

　Ali Obeid

"I like the non-imposing, non-intruding way by which the author is bringing forth his feelings about the Universe, Divine Spirit, profound spiritual (as I would not call it religious) yearnings—and the gentleness that transpires— together with the decisive strength of the feelings expressed. . . . I find this to be a book open to various readings and understandings: it truly encourages one to go beyond his or her current borders and strengths."

　Bogdan Cranganu-Cretu

BOOKS BY THE AUTHOR

Forever Free

This title is available as a free eBook at
WiseWordWind.com.

Falling Into All
Prayer Sayer Song
Rise Eyes Wise

Falling Into All

BEN R. TEETER

WISE
WORD
WIND
PRESS

Wise Word Wind Press
P.O Box 371732
San Diego, CA 92137
WiseWordWind.com

This is not a work of fiction. Names, characters, places, locations and incidents are all real and are meant to bear a relationship to real-life individuals, living and dead, and actual places, business establishments, locations, events and incidents. Any resemblance to the reader and to those he or she may know is entirely intentional.

Cover Art is a painting by Peter Everly, Untitled, Copyright 1988, used by permission.

Cover Design by Randy Gibbs

Book Layout by Golden Ratio Book Design

First Edition

Printed in the United States of America

ISBN: 978-1-7349891-0-6 (Trade Paperback)
ISBN: 978-1-7349891-4-4 (Hardcover)
ISBN: 978-1-7349891-1-3 (Ebook)

Library of Congress Control Number: 2020916079

ACKNOWLEDGMENT

Writing the Word called Today,
It is You.
Only Your ink can penetrate and hold this page.
Only Your Hand can manage this script.
We are the curve of one cipher,
Feeling the moving pen press,
Feeling the deep wetness in the ink,
Feeling You writing us like a river,
The loving touch of pen point to paper,
Moving
Existence
All.

TABLE OF CONTENTS

No, there is no
Table for these Contents
Here to be framed.
No crossroads, signposts, fence,
No places named.
Only drifting grains of
Sand and stars,
Sparkling, scattering in
Wind.
For yourself
Mark places,
If you will.
Set yourself a table.
Let your time be spent
Out here
Within the Loving of this
Wilderness.
Pour wine
From these jars.
Dine.
Be
One
All
Content.

PREFACE

For me,
No saying
Written down
Is worth the small
Black dye
That it may occupy,
That does not
Open
Poor contracted
Mind, heart, eye
To see, to
Be
Some softly open
Sky.

~~~

As we journey,
May your steps lighten
As we join in
This conversation.

—Ben
10/10/10

Let
A   There
Wave   Is
Tip
                     Perfect
On   Peace
The
Surface   In

Of   Falling
The   Into
All-ness   All.

Cease
Frightened
Call.

Falling Into All

Sky
Falls through,
Body erased.
No more
Place.
Where I was,
Graced.

A burst
Of Heart sparks
Showers,
Cascades.
I hug
The Deep Sky
Back.

God's wind
Blows through the
Instrument
Of many holes.
Hard limits
Sing.

Ocean,
You do not teach.
You wash.

You give a wondrous
Taking away.

What appears is a
Lustrous
Disappearing.

Borders,
Shadows
Drop.

Old friends,
Infinite, Nothing, and One
Have a conversation,
Come to understand
Each other and
Stop fighting,
Laugh and laugh.
Enjoying
The moment,
They connect,
And
Merge.

Send crows.
Pick away flesh bits.
Send Sun.
Bleach bone.
Let breezes sing
In a smiling
Chalk rib
Cage,
Empty.

Am I a hill?
Or am I a valley?
I really, really want to know!
An irately inquisitive young
Place
Demands,
Clutching its borders
Around it,
Jealously looking at the other
Rolling green land
All around.

Matrix collapses.
World's tower collapses,
Particles tumbling down
Smaller, smaller,
Smaller still.

And I surrender and
Collapse
This place,
Under the falling, falling
Power
Of the
Grace.

Grace
Drops like rain
Streaking straight down in
Passionate direct hits
In moving swaths
Of pure clear
Life-givingness:

Another parched spot
Gone. Gone!

O,
To stand in the fleet
Sweet falling.
To feel the
Solving, the
Washing
Anew.

And after,
The shimmering,
Shining like dew.

Grace
Drops
Like rain,
Loving
You.

Please permit me
To dust your house
And straighten up
Plump the pillows
Throw out the trash.
Please permit me to
Pull the weeds in
Your garden and
Turn the soil.
I had thought I wanted
To be your Mayor, but
Please, allow me.
Butler, maid, gardener
Is better,
Or, better,
Let me be
The dust
The soil.

Human beings,
Loving sweet,
Launching into
Each others arms,
Falling into each others
Eyes,
Now the vast night skies
Shine all around us
Even in this, the
Daytime.
Falling in upon us
Deeply, deeply, but
Not dissolving,
Holding us here,
Love
Is now so
Clear.

Andrew
On his Path
Serving
With a high powered
Military weapon
In his hand,
Placing his body
In the ways of harm
As an act of
Transcendent love,
While his enemy,
Uttering the Names of God,
Does likewise:
Their great prayers
Rise like fire
From their souls, as
They stalk and shoot,
Cleansing ,

Atoning days,
Settling old debts,
Serving humanity, and
God
Most merciful,
Most Infinite in
Ways.

Ever
Now
New.

Now
Bursts
Here
All.

There Is
Nothing.
But
One.
Infinite.

Your Sages, Saints, a
Bright bouquet of
Humanity's flowers
Rest on the sill of Time in
Eternity's window.
The sweet scent
Fills the Room
With the spaciousness of
Night Sky.
Walls open, drop.
The window sill becomes
A ballroom without walls,
Our breathing,
Time's majestic dance.
We dream a change
Alive.
Your Sages now materialize.
And now in All Earth's
Awakening material, -
Your Eyes.

I sing my birds, I
Soar them
On the breeze.
I push out
My new leaves, and
Cover all the soil with
All my tiny weeds.
I trot, wagging tails,
My dogs.
I breathe my breaths,
I beat my hearts,
I live my lives,
I die my deaths.
I exuberate.
I jubilate.
I exfoliate,
I annihilate.
Ever, I totally
Create.

Urgency has
Wandered away,
Gotten lost, and
Now its energy is busy
Making bird songs
And the feathers of
Life's pillow.

Things un-thing.
World becomes hug.
The Universe embraces, and
The head rests back on
Perfection's pillow.
The body lies on the
Deep featherbed of
Being.
Life sings, as
A chorus of
Morning birds.

We try.
We die.
We fly.
We defy.
We cry.
We sigh.
We
I.

Upon this
Vast water,
I am the ripple
Under the wind's
Tender Hand.
I am the vast water.
I am the wind.
I am the Tenderness
Of the
Touch.

I lift the
Tent flap,
Not to peek out,
But to throw it
Into the sky and
The tent is
Gone.
There is only
Wind
Across a
Crystal sand
Of
Stars.

My self
I make
A perfect
Prayer
And rise up
To the Throne
And sit there long
And sit there
All
Along.

Choose carefully
Your next footstep,
The turning in your path,
The places where
You will arrive.
By choosing
Love,
Here,
You will
Thrive.

I have,
For years,
Been incensed.
And now,
I have been
Incensed.

World, today
We clean the barn
And spread what
Animals have dropped
Upon the field.
Fresh sprouts are
Everywhere, and soft
The scent of Love
As tender fingers green
Embrace the earthen face.

In blazing warmth
The cosmos calls awake
The tender seeds.
Softly rotting,
Last year's remnant
Feeds.

Evolution's swift
Wind
Presses my skin and bones.
Tosses the sea.
Topsie turvies
My decks.
Gyrates
The skies.
I find the
Deck's fulcrum,
The Sea's
Totality.
I find that I
In Sky.
I am the Dance.
I cease to cry.
I leap
Into the Wind.
In stillness,
Fly.

As the quiet safety of
Standing in
Eternal Ground
Brings joyous pleasure in
A sparkling world,
These old mistakes of man
No more disturb than
The erratic air grabbing
Of babies, or the
New plant sprouts
Wandering and waving
Their way into place.
No panic leaping left, today.
Feel the
Beauty
Of the
Way.

In perfectly stable
Total change,
A blackness burns
A very hot cool,
A totally alive
Nothing.
I am held in this
Complete no holding.
I feel it flush me through.
I feel it
Love, so
Nuanced, many fold,
In this no place
I do not occupy.
A breeze upon
A windowsill.
A chin, an elbow, a man,
Strewn through
With wind,

Made, too, of wind.
Only wind.
Burning with
Perfect cold.
A wind from
No place.
Blowing
Still.

Clothing starts
Unwinding and
Floats away,
Silken scraps
Upon the wind.

I feel Earth,
Holding tightly to the
Spinning air,
Never to let go, -
Let go.
And air drifts off.
There is no more blow.
I feel an urge, an urge about
Being in action,
Going.
Gone.

No need to
Evaporate,
Exhale infinitely,
Collapse into
Original particles,
Or sparkles,
Or to
BE
All The Things That Are.

The need factor, the thing factor,
The Be factor, the See factor,
The collapse, evaporate,
And hold-together factors:
All these, seeming Elements
In some wide
Periodic Table tide,
Are a brief moment in a
Fluttering of a flag.
Factor.

O, You. You
Woke me this morning,
Listening
To all my questions
Perfectly,
And guided my mind
To each answer,
An deposited my heart
Into this place of
Joy.

Time:
Take your time.
And when you have it,
Held in your two hands
Like a bubble, or
A great fragile droplet,
A tear,
Release it:
A bubble rises into vast sky.
A teardrop falls
Into a deep and salty sea,
Time spreads
Like a wing
With no
Edge.
Free.

Take a break
From doing,
From being.
Stand between
Everything,
Even rest.
And joy,
And even Peace:
Between
All.
No going needed.
No structure
To hold.
Things surround, and
The brain picks among them
Like a bird beak.
Stand
Between
Some bird pecks,

Unstartled
By vast, vast
All.
No big.
No small.
Between,
Again,
Fall.

The skin
Cools, goes dry,
Blows away,
A scrap of paper
On the wind.
The landscape
Opens wide
Twinkling with lights,
Only
Starry sky.
This face,
Space.

In my dream last night,
I heard you ask
God
To help
The situation.
But, I said,
God is
The situation.

The brightness of
All loving All
Shines in
This person's smile.
This person knows,
Is standing in,
The solid ground
Beyond the trial.

Dear One,
I find here two actions.
I you. (This you is a verb.)
You i. (This i likewise)
There is a rise and a fall
Merged in sweet Yoga, here
Within this tadasana,
This infinite thin spine strand
Wherein I stand.
Two
Washes
In Infinite waves of
One ocean, out to
Our Home,
Nothing.
You murmur to me
In the structures of
Things.
All
Sings.

Asylum in storm,
It is said, is found small
At the point
In the eye.
Oh, no,no. Go. Go
As full storm.
Be all the storm.
For the storm,
Itself,
There is no storm.
In your storm's strong arms
Fly.

Change! Change!
People cry, Change!
Some few say, ...
Changeless!

Givingness
Is poured
Cup to cup, each
Overbrimming.

Plenitude
Without limit,
Floods,
Washes away
All
Cups.

This, too,
Is the Body
Of God.

The fleeting lines of time
Exist only for the hurrying one,
Whose points A and B
Have separated.

There is really
No special costume for this.
No special place.
No words, specific.
No activity, of a type.
There could be some falling
Sawdust, or some greasey rag, or
Moving papers, or dollars, or
Guns, or diapers there at hand,
Or loud songs, or any item else, - At,
within, the Moment
Time ends.
There can be a movie on TV.
A string of cars all lined ahead
Up at the light.
A toilet cool beneath the skin
In still of night...

All
May touch Here,
Anywhere,
And Soul
Cease to fight.

Enjoy the meadow
Galaxy
This tender starry strew of
Wild flowers,
In perfect poised array,
Warmed in Love's Sun this lovely
Infinite Day.

Dare
Let heart pour, as a
Waterfall thundering,
Face wet in the spray,
Rainbow shining in air
Around hair.
Dare, in this way,
Pray.
With Nothing
To say.

You may speak to
Intelligence Infinite Perfect.
Surely This One with us hears
Without flaw.
When awaiting reply,
Drop arrogance, deafening.
Find humility,
The deepest soft.
Open all your skin
With Awe.
This hearing, a dissolving is,
A disappearing, and a
Being only
All.

Under all the plants, the animals,
Is soil, humus, the
Humble, holding up
All feet, secure,
Giving anything each needs,
Accepting anything each drops, and
Melting it away.
Letting each rise forth
Into the day
From within its dark.
With
Nothing at all
To say.

❦

People who are
Strong of will
Often have ideas
Few, simple, shrill of tone,
To which they are aligned, like
River in a canyon's stone
Unstoppable
No matter what
The other people say.

For such,
A pole star, inner, unmoved,
Guides their way,
And, bringing others with them,
They arrive
No matter what,
And, getting there, not resting,
Still they carry on, and strive.
This is just their way.

Time lingers for a while,
And then goes away,
And only one
Vast Moment
Now is Here.
No year.
No tear.
No fear.
O, yes.
They did say
That there would be
Some sort of bliss
Like this
One day.

People
Work and move
Surrounded in a mind
Aflow with daily care
And often seem to miss the
Big Where.
But, notice
Where we are!
Here
I stop and
Stare.

This, our homey neighborhood,
This galaxy, this chakram,
Poised and turning softly in
The body of the
Nothing,
Pouring forth, and
Blossoming,
Immense, sweet life
Beingness,
Is but one
Tiny wild flower
On a
Vast, wide,
Velvet meadow.

Cool and Infinite,
A breeze comes blowing.
Fixity breaks up.
Love flushes through this local
Brain and face.
Heart opens window.
Overflowing here, the breath of
Deepest space
Is crystalline and sheer,
Unmoving, full.
Only elements eternal
Now are here, and
Daily business made of only
Pure generic,
Changeless parts,
As is this person,
Sitting,
Here.
So still.

On permanent vacation,
The Holy Man's heart
A geyser is, of
Freedom's laughter.
Dusty travelers
Gather here and sit
Refreshed, clean, wet,
In the bold peace.
Laughter proliferates
Like tender wild flowers
That spring up
In perfect poised array.
Wounded ones, washed,
Release their tears.
All of their fears
Go soft to sleep.
The hug here
Of the Universe
Is deep.

Raise and open wide the arms
Of your soft innerness.
Open, feel and
Hug huge the
All.
Feel the full
Hug
That you were already in,
Warming and holding you
To the foundation.
Register it on inner skin
And the bones of your breath,
And, Go ahead:
Take it personally.
Feel this hug holding, all through,
Not just your heart,
But each artery, eyelash, sinew,
And all the fine downy feathers
Of your Soul, all
Whole.

The marvel of so many cars,
Tracking together ,
In live speeding flow, and
All of the money bits
Clicking in place, just so, and
All the small packets
In all of the bloods, as they go
Surging and bumping their circuits,
The flavorful whirlings
Of planet and star in their
Passionate dance:
So many marvels, myriad, immense,
Dilute and dense,
Buried right in plain sight in our
Common sense!
Awaken the glories in
This sentience,
Grand, fine.
Notice, feel the amazing
Divine.

Focus, refine, propel forth your
Utter receptivity.
Fiercely will the battle, toward
Your complete surrender.
Fight hard for the most total,
Total loss.
Create, assemble, fabricate a
Dissolving.
Give the biggest possible
Taking in.
Harden yourself in your
Softening.
Write out, unceasing,
Your erasing.
Act in all possible stillness.
Throw the spear of your own
Mortal wounding,
In hostility, huge, of
Tranquility.
Total.

The day's ciphers, letters,
Nouns and pronouns
Drift off
Like dried leaves,
Rattling away and leaving
Wind, only.
The wind stills, reaches, touching
Up past all the stars and
Stands among all particles
And figments, richly
Empty.

Profanity's heat
Tries to drive away
The dread
That it is,
Itself,
Inducing.

I fall
Into
All.

My wealth has
No limits.
I count coins
With kingdoms inside.

My Friend is
Everywhere,
Everyone.

Even the brim
That was overflowing
Is gone.

It rains
Jewels...

The pedestrians
Have all turned
Into angels.

Suffering
Is a fine thread passing
Through a needle of gold.

The fruit is dew fresh,
The table and plates,
Fine and old.

Suddenly,
Here,
Behind my skin,
It is You,
Here with me,
Here as me.
There is
Nothing more
To
Want.

When the skin
Opens to God,
And falls away,
Entirely,
The comfort is
Softer
Than feathers.

Traveler,
Feel this place.
Its heft,
The timbre in
Its voice.
What smile it makes
Within the face
Of its land.
What creases
Crossroad here?
How holds it its sky?
What glories hold its plants?
How pass here the lights and
Shadows of the day?
What does
This place
Say?

Don't be dragged
Off through Death's door,
Bleating as at slaughter.
Take her hand.
Have a chat.
Walk with her as friend.
Become her son or daughter.
Feel even now
The flying feeling
Of your skin and bones,
Drifting off, soft, sure,
Dissolved
Back among the stars.
Into a wind.
Pure.

All is simple
And fully resolved.
It is only we
Who love
To find the half-way
Of everything,
And dangle there
On the jagged
Loose ends
Of the unfinished,
To enjoy the alarm
And excitement.

Let roof
Fly high.
Let wall
Fall.
No floor,
No shoe.
Being only
All.

Truth is there,
Just outside the house.
Go to fresh air.
Soil.
Feel all that this house
Rests in:
The Nurturing All.
Let off the roof.
Let walls fall.
Let foundations
Be wiped away.
Be
Barefoot on the shore of
What Is.
Roof of stars.
Walls of wind.
Floor of
What Is Sure.
No end.

What you can say
Is only a string, passing
From B to A,
Within the Greatness of
Full Day.
Your lines
Of reasoning soon
Shall fade, fall.
Use them only
Tenderly
If at all.

All knows
All.
No pebble
Too small
To toss an ocean into.

There is a rest that is felt
By the blossom
Complete in its bloom.
By the maid,
Shining bright as the stone
On her hand,
As she walks with her man,
Into the waiting family's room.
By the old, old tree,
Standing there, where
It built itself, slowly
Of strong, sweet wood.
By the soul
That discovers the
Brilliance
In which it dwells,
For good.

O, You
Break this moment
On this shore.
As rushing, bursting time
Strikes the rock of space,
You make the moment
Roar.
And then recede
Without a trace.
Into humility's smallest small,
Finally I fall,
And I am
Only You,
All.

In the greatest of
Floods,
Even the stones
Are washed away.

My brain
Smacks me,
Stinging
The side and front of my face,
With its tear
Of hot irritation.
It cannot follow
Here,
Today.
It raises noisey fuss
To stop me going on
Without it,
Ranting on about
Each person, each
Arrangement of events
Encountered,
Cursing
God's Body,
Trying to erase

The Fragrance that
Threatens
To fly it away.

When I hold
Up to Him
This empty skull,
Like a wine cup,
Holding by the stem, thin,
At the heart within,
He pours and fills it up
To the very
Brim.

Stoking the fire of
Loving people,
Just
Toss your dry stick self
Into the firestorm of
Allness
All around us.
Clutching your
Moist life
Tight around you
Will not work here.
So, forget it.
In this circumstance,
You and
Your bark,
Dark
Are all
Dry gunpowder,
Ready for the
Spark.

Let's go now
Into the motions
Of the day.
People to see.
Things to say.
Objects to shift
From place to place.
All
Standing drenched
In the falling
Grace.

My friend,
Are you waiting
For all the lights to come on
In the last moment of death,
To see how you have wasted
Your love?
Why wait for this rude shock,
When you can have it now,
And mend your way?
Your bitter grimace
Hurts your face.
Your plodding footsteps,
Are not bringing forth
Security you seek, and
Greed just makes you more wild.
A near-death experience
Would be just the thing for you,
My child.

When you shift your focus to
Infinity, all around you,
 Like a snow of jewels,
Without surcease,

Instead of a form or two:
A job, a meal, some words,

Then Heart's eye flutters open,
Pouring Gratitude,
Impaled in Peace.

One
Silent Sea
Whispers, rustling here
Against the jewel
Tiny sand-grain skin
Of This,
The beach
Of Being.

Sri Ramakrishna
Cries out with joy
Within the lap of Ma, in bliss,
His tears stream, as
He feels Her squeeze,
Her sweet caress, Her kiss,
'O, Why be One,' he cries,
'When Two
Can feel like this?'

Let
Grace
Of
Being All
Here
Fall.

The bird bursts
Into morning song,
Having waited
All night
Long.

This day,
This moment
Spills
And pours, so
Like a ruptured sack,
And all of time's sweet
Shining, fragrant grain
Goes sliding,
Falling
Out
Away.

I went to where
The oaks are old,
And, older, still
The boulders gray.
The evening sky
Grew night,
And then, behold:
Poised, here at hand,
The graceful, bright, grand
Milky Way.
And there was
Nothing
Else
To say.

There is a
Rich and winy
Complex smell
That lingers
In the chaparral,
Soothing,
Saying,
All is well.

I lay me down
Within Your river bed,
And mingle softly
Perfect
In Your flow
With no resistance to
The twisting banks
Of being,
So, I come to know
The feelings of
A Comfort After Happiness.
A
Perfect
Thanks.

And here, this
Teeming coffee shop,
This
Temple
On a busy street
Up rises, dearly,
Like a mountain top
Into the spacey Sky, so sweet,
And clearly
Here is only Earth and Sky,
And I, in long
And peaceful solitude
At song.

How did so many men get started
Believing themselves to be subject
To the brain and gene,
Rather than
Their composer?
All the dancing
Lights and colors
Moving in the living cell,
Not our weather sky,
But our handwriting,
Our own
Word
To tell.

In the day's work,
In the face of this client,
And those of the others working,
In the tools,
And their motions,
In the product,
In the dream
Of the product,
There is You,
So alive and lovely,
So deeply
Quiet.

Here,
Two eyebrows arch
Over two clear windows.
Inside,
A soaring sanctuary of
Love.
Under this roof,
Thatched with some hair,
We silently meet.
The place, the moment, the air
Sanctified.
Still.

Infinity
Blows It's breeze
Through the branches
Of this body's
Forest of trees
And flutters all
It's leaves.

The atoms
Where I'm sitting
Swell and glow
With song.
Their joyous
Oscillations
Cymbal, gong.
There is a brightness
Like a dawn.
And an Ocean
Full of comfort, and
This small note-taker
Gone.

No disaster
This Flood,
Though all
Is gone -
The house,
The personal things.
This long-sought
Flood
No sorrow
Brings.

Sweet Infinity beckons, then
Bathes
The moment,
And I,
And the other
Personal pronouns
Are all washed away.
Love,
In this Infinitude,
Is quiet.
The still joy,
Deep
At the foundation of Being,
Is the reason why, even the
Most boisterously miserable man
Clutches to Life,
Imagining that This
Might leave him,
Or he
Depart from It.

The head meanders
Back into minutia,
Collecting, collecting, and Forgetting
All.
Mercy, prevailing,
Over-floods the banks,
Again,
And all my
Personal stuff
Is soaked.
It is
A happy day.

When the moment is OK,

When the second is
Seriously wonderful,

When the instant burgeons
With newly broken frontiers
Of Gratitude,

And when the very Point of
Being
Sticks you to the core, and
You
Scream
Joy,
In absolute, absolute
Silence,
Yes.
It is a nice day.

These great red rocks
Striped and so slowly tumbling,
The most slow and vast
Second hand moving
Around here,
Make mute monuments
To movements that
Only a planet
Might record,
Remember.
This volume of
Flat pages,
Here fallen open,
Speaks open
All
Time.

How amazing and mysterious,
That You
Have become
Beings
Such as we,
So bright on fire,
In seeming flaw,
And lost,
So much of time,
To
Awe.

Hard layers deep
Of silent stones
That lie asleep
A mile
Below our feet,
A test
To times gone,
Years
A billion long,
And this
Already in
The middle
Of the song.

Behold

The hold
Of Nature's
Nurturing hug,
So sweet
So long
So deep.
She will
Awaken you
When you are done
With sleep.

World,
You wear
The frown of fear
While resting on
The shore of Peace,
Love's Ocean
Roaring
In your ear.

It is time
For the
Timeless.

Let
Cry
Die.

This
Starlight dust bunny
We float on
In this Sky
Gathers its
Strings and knots
Tightly, lest
They blow away,
Engulfed in
Rapture
In this Deep.

Only a few
Rare ones
Dare
To test the limits of
Human sweetness,
And go beyond
Home's bond
And village pale
Of friendly old connection
So to scale
An Everest of Love, or
Walk a Moon,
Full and silvery
Bright, of Joy, or steep
Descend the Ocean deep,
And lie down in It's bed,
Pressed, caressed,
Drowned away.

Only a few
Come here
To stop
To stay.

The day is filled, so,
With His care,
There is no room
For more new prayer.
For He is here
So close,
Already All,
There is no space
To reach
Or call.

Knowing nothing,
Mind a blank,
I step full forward
On Your Plain
Beneath Your Sky,
And follow forth Your
Compass line,
Carefree.
And if confusion
Should arise
Upon a matter
Small or great,
I open arms
And feel you here
Administrate
So perfectly.

Why should I
Interfere?

All

(is)

Nothing

(but)

Infinite

One.

There is all the changing of hands
Of things, and all the
Noise, the excitement, that
All that brings, and
Then it stops, and
Eye and hand, their
Restlessnesses
Cease, and
Counting and containers
Disappear.
There is a chance
To let the mind
Go still and clear,
Go falling off
The Earth,
Go falling out
Into Deep Sky.
And know again that
All
Is
I.

The cipher
We name Nothing
Takes its stand
Among the other numbers,
No more grand.
Yet there are times
It seems to seek
To stage a coup,
To be the very
Home, the
Prince of
All.
This is really, simply
Nothing
New.
Then, once again
This figure takes its fall
And disappears
Among the other numbers,
All.

Like a soft
Cashmere coat,
This World,
Spun and woven
Of all Your loves
Holds and warms and
Comforts, and
Fits like
Softest
Gloves.

Underfoot,
The rocky soils
Live their days
In year millions.
Overhead,
The twinkling worlds of lights
In billions.
Or so,
In this moment
Of almost no breadth,
A passing artifact
Of thought
Imagines.

Beached
Under Your
Sky,
A strand,
Here,
I lie.

Wisp,
Fly!

Let
Dawn begin.
Let evening end.
Let time, let
Wisp of mind
Flow.
Let knowledge
Know.
Let seed
Sow.
Let going
Go.
Let this wisp
Whisper,
...O.

It is the dark evening of the year,
And the dark dawn of the year.
Time is changing clothes,
About to wear new numbers.
The harvest has been great,
The moments of love are piled high
In the heart's granary,
Like a mountain.
The seed bag, heavy, is poised
To pour forth freshness,
Love's fountain.
Evening, dawn,
Old harvest, new seed,
How can this mind distinguish?
No need.
Your fragrant golden grain
Pours and pours.
The granary
Is buried.

Love
Flower petals blow softly open
One by one
From this heart
And gradually surround me.
God's great bee buzzes, lands,
Crawls inside this core,
Aroar.
The tender fingers and eyes
Of all things
Start giving me their touches.
Want becomes
The deep hug of trust.
Listen. You can hear
The conversations and the singing
In the fields
Of stars.

And Mind,
Long fond of
Dark surmises,
Stops
Its foolish bet,
For yet,
Again,
It cuts away
Its own safety net,
Only to fall,
Fall
Into the soft,
Soft, soft
Ground
Of
All.

I sit
To write You a note
And feel
All,
Around me,
And I am gripped
In Your hand
As I grip the pencil, and
Writing happens.
But there is no one
Elsewhere
To write to.
Only a song of love
Going on.

Another day
Circles its sweet round,
Shimmering light,
Moving air, water,
Plants, animals,
A mix of human
Working sound.
Some hours awake
Between sleeps.
The blue bead sparkles
As it turns its way,
In a jeweled necklace
On the velvet deeps.
Another day passes, scintillate,
Evanescent, brilliant, intricate,
Profound, Infinite, non-separate
In One
All.
Another day
For Awe.

In that moment
When every word
Burn
Like dry tinder
And there is heard
One Silence-Full,
Holding all Reality
In its depths,
And every kind
Of every object
You may find,
Is singing like
A bird in throng
A simple, simple song
It did not need to learn,
In this moment,
Time itself, also
Softly
Burn.

Ripples gurgle
In a stream
And pass so quick
Away,
So like this thought,
This moment
Now.
So like
This day.

Dwell
Here,
Where there is only simple truth.
No speculative bubbles
Making important, lengths of time and
Quantities of space, and
Making certain items seem to
Have great worth.
Dwell here, where there is
Nary any height or length or girth,
And time has lost its rush,
And all things equally are
At their death
Or birth.

There is a sudden failure of
Suffering, and
We have a collapse
In the economy
Of ache and pain,
Followed by heavy rain
Of sunny gold Grace
Washing away all
The structures of shadows,
Leaving no trace,
No stain.

I open for You
This empty page,
And place it where
I hope you will walk,
Hoping for a dust particle,
Or smudge, or slight
Impression from Your foot,
Which will make my heart
Shimmer all day.

Suddenly
The money is everywhere
Gone.
The medium of flight
Left everyone
Who was on it, borne,
Fluttering
Their little wings
Like baby angels
Looking for God.
The solid ground
On which we trod
Evaporated so
Quickly.
Is it not odd?
This free fall feeling
That we share,
Dropping together in the air,
Has us seeking some

New ground
On which to stand.
We, strangely, now, cannot
Climb and stand
Upon each other.
Where, we wonder, is
True
Solid land?
Fall, fall we all,
Perhaps to find at last some
Footing
Waiting for us all along.

Let us enjoy,
Let us glide
This route
To that place
Of
No more doubt.

A catalytic chemical,
A leaf of subtle spice
Tossed in the kettle,
Nice.
A tiny corner of the world
Where just one heart
Sits now aglow:
Small things, we know, can
Purify the burning,
Elevate the savor,
Energize a World's eye
To feel
A possibility
And grow.

Sometimes it's nice to
Let a busy mind
Lie down and die,
And place an empty funnel
From the heart
Up straight
To empty sky
And wait.

Teach me,
O, Silent One,
To stretch my soul
Like softest skin
Upon a drum,
To feel Your gentle pounding,
And to be resounding
This All
As it may come.

Feel the press
And deep caress,
The hug of gravity,
Sublime,
That holds each
Being
In its own sweet
Space and time.

Become the
Dark
Night
Sky.
And then,
Squeezing this fruit,
The black Ink
In which
All things
Are written.

As a child, playing barefoot,
Or maybe I was working,
Getting cows, in the upper pasture,
Where the thorn bushes grow,
Fine, spaced, hard wood bushes
Bristling with shiny, gray, straight,
Razor sharp thorns, an inch long,
I somehow obtained one:
A black, perfect dot
In the center of my sole.
For more than a week
I limped over this
Small black dot, waiting.
Finally it festered soft.
Out it came, astonishingly
Long, smooth, sharp, perfect,
Its mission executed
Without flaw.
I was
In awe.

At a touch
Of Infiniteness,
Time rings
Like a bell.
And Space
Grows silent
To hear
What It has
To tell.

This
Silent temple
Heart
Of mine,
Wherein I sit
To hear the morning hymn
Divine,
Sequestered
In a special
Place and time
Of day and week.
This golden coin
You dropped
Into this beggar's cup,
Far richer than
I thought to seek.
I am All
Filled up.

This heart of mine,
This bowl,
Stands empty. No,
So open wide,
It holds only
All
The Sky.

Feeling fragments
Fit as One,
I find,
Life is so wise,
I see
That it is You,
Laughing
In It All,
Teasing wisdom out
Into the open.

Open.
Open
Me more,
Like a door,
I implore.
Let me
Only be
Only to
Adore.

Each shining
Fragment
Fits so
Sure.
So
Pure.

As You
Move in
Behind my eye,
There ceases to exist
A 'my.'
And You or I
Sing Grace
Into this world, and
Falling into All,
Where all the pronouns'
Held positions fail,
There is no I,
Nor You, nor He, nor She, nor We
To mark a trail.

Do remember,
Dry one,
That the path to the well, deep,
That you need, that you seek,
Starts
In the palm of your hand,
And leads right inside
To your Heart.
Immerse
To the eyes, and
See the Wonder
Everywhere.
Wash away
Mind's lies.
Be stunned
By the glittering
Jeweled light,
The beauty of normal things,
The very act
Of sight.

Existence and I
Have come to
Care for each other
Like old love birds,
With routines and
Surprises
All designed to
Nurture and please.
We murmur sweet thoughts
In each others' ear,
Laughing, hugging each other.
I so enjoy when dear
Existence
Presents me some itch on the back
For me to scratch, or
Some pain to ease.
And Existence
Has my back covered
With ease.

A sprig
In the pot
Changes
The meal
A lot.

I pause, poised here
Among these solids,
Liquids, gases, in this
Haze of waves
Upon this
Cooled down
Piece of star,
In streaming coils
Of common chemical
Made musical,
Here, far
From warmer, brighter
Hearts of life
Seen strewn
Across the Way.

I pause and ponder,
Deep in this deep
Pool of Love,

How nice it is to waken
Here today.
I snuggle deeper,
Deep into your holding Arm,
And, gazing like a baby,
Giggle at your jingling trinkets,
Feeling solid, soft, and
Warm.

Move aside,
Worries.
Make room for the relief
Of
Reality.
The sweetness
Of which is so
Beyond
Your belief.
Your world of
Bad case scenarios
Requires a
Fragile shroud of
Ignorance
To exist,
Yet,
So loving drama,
You persist.

I say,
Move aside.
Go.
And take with you,
Your friend, Risk.
If you guys stay,
You won't last long.
You will be drowned,
And not be missed,
In these depths,
Reality.
Blissed.

May I make
This wordy mind
An ear,
A telephone,
A listening,
That I may find
And hear
Precisely
What You have to say
To me today?

Please, remember
You are 100%
Divine.
You are never, ever unsafe.
So, relax.
Love.
There is no need
For anything else.
And, please,
Love your friends,
And don't worry, so.
This all goes for them,
100%,
Also.

Below all
The breaking, Your
Being,
Bedrock.

You are,
Not just conscious,
But Perfect
Intelligence.
You are,
Not just happy,
Or even thrilled,
Or even joyous
In love,
But You are only
All
Love.

I whisper
Into the quiet megaphone
Of your heart,
My Humanity,
My Love.
Do You hear Me?
It is the sound of
Soft falling rain
Upon the dryness
Of long parched
Pain.

May that I make
This wordy mind
An ear,
A telephone,
A listening,
That I may find
And hear
Precisely
What You have to say
To me today.

Directed by You,
Silent One,
I have no idea
Where I go next.
I know only, I am
Here.
And I am falling,
Falling
Into arms,
Your arms of Time,
Falling into Love,
And each fresh
Precipice
A gift.
And so this falling feels,
At times, more like
A lift
From up, way up
Above.

Hold a sky
Of reverence, soft
Around the planet
Of your Being,
Like a dawn,
A sunset,
An aurora borealis,
Sparkling, glowing, warm
Around your form.
And you will find
You sing and call
With other birds,
Unseen, but of
Your feather,
Prayer sayer,
In the Vastness
Of this All,
O,
Lovely One.

Divine One,
Stand awake, there,
Please.
Do not forget,
Again,
That which You are,
And where You are.
Please do not
Create Yourself
A small angry animal,
Again, O,
Merciful One,
Creator of Heaven,
Lover of All,
Divine One.
Please,
Stand there,
Tested,
Tall.

Change
Breaks up
Firm whole things
Into
Unfitting pieces,
Floating
Without a place,
Struggling
To reassemble
Somewhat like they were,
But never done,
Until
Love takes them,
Holds them all,
And they can
Melt again
Into the
One.

As the Divine One,
That you are,
My friend,
You can be
Anywhere,
Anything.
And You can change Your choice
Anytime.
You can make
Where You are
Solid or soft.
You can
Flick the light
On and off.
Hold out Your hand.
Have roses or thorn.
No need to develop this.
This
Is how You were born.

You give me
The glittering pour
Of Your
Prosperous
Infinity.
You give me
The beautiful
Nothing
Of the
Free.

Some of us will
Sit and whine
Even as we,
In all comfort,
Dress, or dine,
About a lessening
Of good,
When a great
Lessoning
One could
Acquire,
Overflowing,
If one would.

As you see
All the varied
Time particles
You can be,
Forget not to
Imbibe,
Be
Sweet
Eternity.

As you see
All the
Oppositions
You can be,
Forget not
To imbibe,
Be
Sweet Truth,
Glorious,
And lose all
Enmity.

Where Silence
Is being
Heard,
Loved,
It rushes in,
Touches,
Engages
In the
Impossible
Friendship.

If I might rise
Into the skies
And see the world
From heightened eyes,
How soft, serene and smooth
It all would seem to glow.

In turning time, the
Air and water,
Rock and living things,
The sketch of Man's
All-populous creations
Smoothly
Come and go.

Words
Dropping on a page
Can be like leaves
And pods of seed,
All dried up,
At a finished stage,
Cast off,
Not, at the moment,
Meeting any need.

Words lifted later
From the page
Under a warming
Understanding stare,
Might open, blossom,
Fragrantly alive, and,
Once again awake,
Aware,
Be freed.

I am the
Silent, soft, and
Perfect
Hug that holds
All
Things,
And to each,
Its own sweet
Effervescent being
Brings.
Soft as the
Soft Eternity,
I hold you in
One
Perfect Love
Down to your
Very core,
Where Love, loved,
Erupts ever more.

I lie flattened back
Against the planet's face,
And feel the great
Soft kiss of gravity
Pressing down upon me,
And our race, and,
With this delicate caress,
You hold us, quietly,
Almost unnoticed,
And I must confess,
So deeply do You bless,
Holding, hugging us
In this, our
Grace filled form,
That I
Forget to notice.
It is such
The norm.

The
Thank You
Grows,
Crescendos,
Bursts,
Goes.
Then goes the me,
And then the
You,
Goes,
Too.

Polished
The wooden grain
And marble vein
In infinite varying
Diversity,
Mysterious in
Harmony,
These only speak
Your Name.

Grand,
The garment green
Of poised leaf, each
So fragrant, sweet, seen
Everywhere, with
Blossom bower, all,
Each countless
Awesome flower, small,
A delicate palatial hall,

These sing
Your Name.

Deep,
The melodious bones
Of multicolored
Many-layered stones.

High,
The brilliant air,
Ever-changing color, shape,
In cool and flame,
In the shining sky
Entrancing,
Dance
Your Name.

Wild,
The animal,
Fish, bird, mammal,
Microbe, insect, all

Of heart shy.
Bright of eye,
All cry
Your Name.

Jewel lace,
The shining heart
Of human race,
In multi-scintillating light,
The deep and dark,
The quiet lustrous, and
The dazzling bright,
Each vibrantly alive,
And, knowingly or not,
So free,
All these,
So differently
And so same,
All speak
Your Name.

With arms as wings
Of golden Love like sun,
He holds so tight your heart
In such an awesome power,
Yet softer and more delicate
Than any tender flower.

The Universe is trembling
To life
This hour.

Here is
A pause,
A moment
At the start of day
To feel
Reality
Self
You.
And try to say,
Somehow,
A song of word.
To sing and soar
In morning
Like a bird.

Full Eye
Of Soul's skin
Feels only
Heaven's
Aware
Still
Wind.

Stumbling,
The moth
Came,
Entered,
Became
Only
Naked
Flame.

There is
Within you
A unique way
To be Divine,
For you alone
To find.

In just
A few moments more,
The body will be dead, rotten,
And all the old good things
Spread upon the lawn to sell
For a quarter or a dollar,
And soon afterward,
Friends gone, name forgotten.

This moment, unrelenting,
Rushes rapidly this way,
Like an arrow, swift, sure,
On course,
It strikes,
Pure. Feel it
Today.

I spread this self
Before You,
Open to a page
Of moments written
In an earlier stage.
I feel your soft eraser
Rubbing out a space
Where things were
Bunched together
Feeling somewhat messed.
I feel Your
Smoothly gliding,
Soothing, guiding
Rewrite
Leaving me feel
New
Blessed.

Cleanly
Split in two,
I find
A shower of You
Stands silent
In my midst.
I cannot touch now
Those old halves.

Somehow, naturally,
These pieced flagstones
Of my numerous
Inevitable mistakes,
Fit perfectly
To make a path,
Clear, flat, wide,
To You.

New.
New page.
New moment.
Newness
Never fails.
Always arrives
In
Time.
Always forgiving.
Always offering.
Always beckoning
To me, to you,
To go.
Be new.

I touch You and
All
Walls
Fall.
My heart free
In
Infinity.
Here
In this chair
The problems
I have composed
Dissolve
Into the
Shimmering air.
Below
Above
One
In
Love.

I read of a Saint in India,
In a culture where
Such things
Don't get you arrested,
Who decided to reach up
To touch You.
As I remember it,
His arm was firmly upraised
For more than twenty years,
And a
Pillar of Blessing
To all
Who saw
Or heard,
As I am blessed
Now.
In gratitude,
I bow.

The dawn glides
Swiftly sideways,
Day by day,
On horizon's line,
As seasons
Fly like hours,
Years like days,
And clock faces
Start to flutter
Like hummingbird wings.
Time explodes
With ripening leaves,
And blooming flowers,
And human lives,
And all the things we know
That burst with life
And go.

Sometimes this
Peevish creature,
Barking like an
Angry dog
Defending its yard,
Tries to chase You out.
Ha!
Try, little pup, to
Chase out the wind
Of your own barking
Breath.

Words
Land here
Like a quick
Flock of birds,
Together.
In song,
From
Sky.
Calling out.
Digging, picking
For fresh feed
Among the rock
And weed.

No matter
How much poverty
I try to create,
I fail at it
Under the Infinite
Pouring bucket
Of Your
All.

Heaven, oh!
Here You are!
Funny,
The map showed You
Further along than this,
Or else,
We made good time.

Look, Honey!
Here it is:
Bliss.

The Time we feel, so
Flowing like a river,
Could encounter,
Might it not?
A waterfall, majestic,
Rainbowed, white, tall,
A sudden roaring
Into
All.

And so this
Age of oil,
So brief,
Shall quickly burn,
And pass away.
And something else,
Some soft surprise
Arrives.
What will it be?
What will we
Learn
Today?

Time
Drops.
Mind's froth
Pops.
Even space
Stops.
This
Empty
Brings
Deep
Smile.
Pause
Here
A
While.

I lie back
Into the
Featherbed
Of Your
Peace.
And in the
Depths
Of gratitude,
You make
Me the
Featherbed.
Your
Peace.

Sometimes, You
Blow the door
Right off its hinges.
Then you blow away
The walls
Into the skies,
Vast and starry,
And,
What a big surprise.
For, though it is not small,
It is quite
Soft and cozy
Here
Among the

All.

And God said,
Let there be
Love.
And there was Love.
And Love permeated all,
Without exception.
And this Love held
Intelligence, brilliant,
Without error or flaw,
Also permeating all.
And God saw
It was good.
And
All stood
In Awe.

And in this joy
God started
To dance and to play,
Turning and turning,
And this was the start
Of the night and the day.
And all God's
Revolving and dancing
In turnings diverse
Spun out things
That were
Yearning, learning,
Evolving,
The sweet
Universe.

Lost one,
Ask.
There is guidance.
Starveling,
Ask.
There is nurturance.
Cold one,
Ask.
Unloved one,
Ask.
Fearful one,
Tortured one,
Diseased one,
Crashing one,
Poor one,
Ask, all.
You are the phone.
Call.

Later,
We find
That beauteous things
Happened quietly,
Unknown to us
In our midst.
And the
Civilization
That we were
Tracking,
Perhaps,
Did not necessarily
Exist.

Try
Gratitude,
And you
Decorate your world
With jewels and
Fill it with doorways.

Go into
Fear,
And you will
Shrink your world
Within
Dark prison bars,
And find
Grim cell keepers
All around you.

It is amazing.

The spigot for
Your weather
Is in
Your heart
With your
Hand on it.

Unless,
You have given it,
Somehow, to
Some
Elusive stranger.

I saw You
Drop, shining,
Into my face,
So it became
Your Sky,
Shining full
From the Heart below,
Some Sky
In a cup.
Pouring
Up.

Infinitudes
Enfold,
Hold,
Where
Gratitudes
Unfold.

Behold.

The bottom
Dropped out
Of the treasure box,
As you hurried,
And the hoard
Tumbled away
With all your
Shining dreams.
You stood
Clutching
A broken box.
Wishing
It were not so.
Your shadow
Stands there still,
Shocked mouth
Frozen
In 'Oh.'

As we say, the
Day breaks,
So sometimes, the
Life breaks.

Being
With all Its
Logic of Love
Opens It's Eye,
And this, another
Human body, a
Fragrant flower
Within this
Sweet Seeing,
Makes.

How many are there
Among us,
Seemingly,
Normally consumed
In small self interests,
Going about the day
Immersed in tasks
About food, clothing, shelter,
Only,
Who secretly,
Frequently fly,
Aloft,
Becoming sweet,
Soft Sky?

Tranquil,
I rest in
All things,
As my clothing.
Things ordinary,
My jewelry.
Things multitudinous,
My waving hair.
All Things
Lightly
I wear.

Reality
Drops burning
Through this
Personality,
Leaving only the
Generic
Eternal
Properties.

Skilled ignorers
That we are,
We are able to
Focus within pittances
In worry
While our lives are
Clothed in
Infinite cascading draperies,
Life's unbounded beauties,
Housed in
The exalted infinite hall
Of the day and the night,
Fed by
The One
Whose hand holds
All.

Time,
Seen to be
Only a
Circularity,
Requiring but a
Point
Of reference,
Becomes
A simple product of
Geometry.
A relic,
Like a shadow,
Relative,
Residing anywhere,
Everywhere
In the eye of
It's beholder.

Time keeper,
Do you
Ride relentlessly
The ever-moving
Spear point
Flying ever forward
At circumference?
Or are you
Making a point
Of
Being
At center?
Do you sometimes
Abandon altogether
Face, number,
Rotating hands,
Point winking out?
Do you sometimes
Lay the
Hourglass
On its side,...

All its sands
At rest?
Perhaps, you've known
These times of
No time
As the best.

☙

A bit of protoplasm,
Carbon chemistry,
Wriggles here
Upon the watery smear
Of a turning sphere,
Measuring the day,
The year,
Struggling, yearning,
Learning
To be free.
Clear.

The herd moves slow,
Each bovine member,
Passive, adds its
Moos and moans, and
Stumbles, groans.
Hooves tap and click
Upon the stones.
Calves frolic, say
"Bah-hah-hah!
Beautiful day!"
Then join again,
Grown serious,
Among
Herd's sway.

Reality
Reels me in
From the chimera sea,
Kicking and flopping.
Resistance becomes
Surrender, then
Whole heartedness.
Storms cease.
That, that is, is
My clothing.
Gorgeousness pours.
I am
Peace.

Blessed are the meek,
For,
Losing all wall,
They fall,
Fall,
Fall
Into the
All.

The time comes
When there is
No time,
For it has
Dropped
Out of existence,
Becoming
Something else,
Or joined
In all its seeming parts
Becoming a
Oneness,
Where days and nights
And seasons,
Dawns and evenings,
Births and deaths
All linger together
In easy conversation,

No longer
Apart.
The time comes
When there is
No time.
All the circularities
In the clock
Having no teeth,
Their centers,
One.

As
Love
Is not something you seek,
But something you do,
And then,
Everywhere
You find,
So
With this feeling,
This knowing, this ambiance
That
All
Is
Aware, Loving, Divine.
It is not in hunting
Among crowded utterances
Of men that you find
Such a Sanctuary, kind,

But in letting go
The prison bars
That you hold,
Fashioning
Yourself,
In your own hands,
Ambiance,
Heart,
Mind.

Morning warms.
You, Reality,
Call me
Into your
All-accepting arms
And I am You,
Unseparated
Again.

You
Drop in
And burn a hole
In my day,
Taking
All time
Away.

Ignited moment,
Stay.

Great
One
Touches.
Soul grows
Still, clear.
Not a babbling brook, now,
But a single drop of
Dew,
Perfect sphere,
Touching each direction,
Holding in reflection
All
Here.

Now
Poised,
Feel
Soul's skin
Touch
Here.
All.

Dances of Love
You have given us,
That we do,
Intoxicated,
Abandoned,
Unwitting,
Unwilling to stop.
The music plays in the air
Between
Man and woman,
Child and parent,
Teacher, student,
Brother, sister,
Friend and friend,
And kind strangers,
Directing our
Footsteps,
In Love
Without end.

Suddenly
Little tubules open
In my body
And the sweet breeze
Of Your silent
Infinite breath
Comes through,
Instantly
Sweeping away
Trouble,
Rendering it
Divine jewels
Of Your Beingness.
A miraculous shift
In perspective
And I am lodged
In Peace,
The stars my
Ornaments,

Perfection,
Completeness,
My pillows.

This good
Fortune
Needs no
Accounting.

Someone attempts
A ledger, to count
The riches of life.
Some income, a few
Spectacular sensations
Get recorded.
But quickly enough,
The Asset category
Explodes,
Taking away
All possibility of
Measurement,
Along with the
Measurer.
Wealth spills
Everywhere.

Even the hands
Reaching to catch it
Fall away
Turned to
Diamonds and
Gold.
The heart's purse
Pours Gratitude
Too vast
To hold.

Burst
Bright
Cascading
Spark.

So,
If you find
That love is blind,
Examine what you love.
Perhaps a different Lover
Might
Restore
Your sight.

A moment out of time
Has come.
Tumbling numbers,
Dropping,
Click into a sum.
The ever-moving
Winds of need
Cease.
All the
Wars
Have paused in
Peace.

The Sky has descended,
Filling the stones and rivers
And all the things and creatures.
No need now to
Fly up.

Up
Is now completely
Among us.

Marks are collecting
In a writing book,
Perhaps to be forgotten,
Never seen,
Or maybe, some day
Someone else
Will take a look.
No matter now,
For me,
The soul a shining moon,
The Self a sky,
The mind a
Babbling brook.

Being
Comes already
Filled
With Truth.
And all the small
Discoveries
Reflected in
The watery weakness
Of a human head
Do not approximate.
Better to relinquish
Fuzzy photos, all,
Instead.
And if you do not try
To pry at Truth,
But when Its simple
Surface skin you find
Before the eye of mind,
Just give It all your

Heart's soft kiss,
Knowing Love
May carry you away
To lie upon
Truth's bed
Of Bliss.

❦

I want money.
I want fame.
I want all who are to come
To know my name.
I want all
To sing my words, so long,
That they preserve a tongue,
To study, after it is gone,
Just
To hear my song.

Let us cast away the
Arrogant dullness
Holding us asleep
To what
Surrounds,
Abounds around us.
Let us shuffle off
This heavy, dark,
Hypnotic pall
That locks us all.
Let us fly free
By noticing
That all this Be
Is made of Love
And full of
Perfect See.
And we
Are also All.
Not merely
Little
Me.

You claim your beauty,
Lovely princess girl,
And play it
As your rightful toy
To rule your world,
Or catch a boy.

But , see
The signature
Upon the form
You claim.
See Whose truly is the
Only Name.

I see you are a citizen
Of this town. So nice.
And a natural citizen, too,
Of this sweet Earth.
Of course you are, born and bred.
And, too, you are a native of this
Local circle, planets, sun.
Around here were you born,
And here you dwell today.
And, as I understand,
This is your local spot,
These local parts, this bright
Galactic Milky Way.
And so, it seems this is
Your local State, wherein
You live and work and play,
How lovely, this,
'The Universe,'
As many of you locals say.

Once again, I feel Your
Total Bigness
Surrounding this, a
Bit of skin and bone,
Holding, nudging,
Making time move.
This little knot
Of coincidences
That You have tied
To make a 'me' aware here,
Tugged,
Holds, like a
Tethered kite.
It could
Unravel
Anytime You want,
Wisps into Wind,
Big,
Letting go
Without a fight.

❦

Awakener,
Sit down
Anywhere.
And if you
Array your attention
Into the Life
Around you,
Open to the true
Magnitude, -
Blessed, meek,
You will dissolve
As It begins
To Speak.

❦

Calamity awakens a
Stubbornly content sleeper.
Purpose lies there,
Deeper.

Look at how

Amazing

Every part of what is, is:
Your arm,
A finger,
A fingernail.
Any item around us,
However odd.

Be stunned, stunned

By the beauty, and
Know
That
All is God.

You are dressed in
That exquisite material,
Your beautiful attention.
Please notice, Sweet One.
See how it molds, shapes,
Sharpens, broadens,
Occupies
Any size.
And what it does daily
Becomes that, that is true,
About and for, you.
And so you might consider,
It might be wise
Taking it out for a
Daily stretch,
Some exercise.

Discovering that your own
Attention frees,
Can take you, make you
Anywhere,
Please,
Free one, please,
Open eyes.
Place it somewhere
Awesome,
Wise.

Living, Loving,
Seeing, Shining
Light Divine
Fills this world
Completely,
Every nook and nugget,
Great or fine.

How is it
Man forgets to see
And learns instead
To moan and groan and whine?

All is amazing,
And, when, at last,
The drama's done,
So kind.

Let us have a
Spicy moment now!
A feisty fight!
Disapproving, scorning
What has happened,
Let us roar out
Judgements,
Sending up a
Smoke of curses
Feeling oh so right!
Barking as a pack of dogs,
Drunken on our hormone cocktail,
Flooding us with
Fight or flight,
Let us cast away our
Loving view,
Rejoicing in the joys of
Being hot and very much
Askew!
Woo Hoo!   All right!

This is serious,
Forgetful one,
Losing your keys.
Here they are,
The jingling joys
You sought,
As you were
Tearing the place apart,
Safe there,
In your
Heart.

꽃

An ant, overwhelmed,
Makes off with
A grain of cake
From an
Unimaginable table.

꽃

A moment of joy
Is a mansion
Full of fine things,
And a garage
With a wonderful car,
Right here,
Where
You are.

✾

Thought, sing.
Mind, ride
Soul's wing.
Self,
Be
All thing.

✾

This flesh,
These bones,
A scattering array
Of jewel stones,
Dissolve away
Among the shining
Sidewalk particles,
And dancing sparkles

In the air, and then
Among the turning planet's
Flash of night, day,
And then in Sun's
Brilliantly abursting star,
Still only just a faint
Reflecting glint of
That
Of Brightness, greater, far.
This flesh,
These bones,
Sitting here,

Flash
Just once
Clear.

Over the hill,
See the
Full moon rise,
Big, bright, round,
Perfect,
Showering calm
Upon the eyes,
Poised
In radiant glow
Upon night's wheel.
Pause, busy one,
Feel.

Mesmerized
Into seeing only
This one swollen
Moment of time,

This hour, day, lifetime,
We are gifted
With such an exquisite
Blindness.
We have the immense capacity
To ignore
The vast numbers
Of minutes, hours, lifetimes,
That surround us here
In this sea of
Time, and beings,
Stretching huge
All around us,
Bobbing with us, together,
In this one same
Warm wave,
Out in a
Colossal darkness that
We have created,
Each,
Around ourselves.

I walk
Toward mirage.
I arrive at
Reality.
Goals fall,
Disappear,
Along with mind.
Nowhere to go, when
Here is
All.

Let us
Go and dance
Upon the roof
Of the world.
Let us
Bend like sky
Over all,
Covering all
With deepest
Love.
Let us stand
At Sky
Most High,
And give
 All
A kiss
In this,
Bliss.

Preparations,
Unneeded,
Fold,
Gone from my head.
Even
The funeral
Is already over.
I am buried in this
Soil,
Being.
You are my
Food, Shelter, Water,
Bed.

Death comes.
Quickly flesh returns
To dust and clay.
All the fuzzy thoughts
Fade away.
Memory, relationship,
Effect, result,
None can stay.
Only
One
Remains,
And This
Available today.

The Old One said,
"I have taken the
Side paths.
My experience broadened.
My sense of the
Narrow true
Clarified.
My mercy
Sweetened.
I have
Burst enough
Illusion bubbles
With the pinpoint
Of Oneness, in
Love's hand, so only
Mercy abounds.

Stumble through
Rock and thorn
A few times, and
Then you appreciate
This old
Road of Being,
So well worn."

This warm
Mammal mortal,
Constant error prone,
Hungers, ever,
Seeks Your
Allness
Oneness
Throne,
Hungry to
The very bone.

Soul alone,
This flickering
Inconstant one
Moves from light
To light to light,
Like moth to flame
To quench, extinguish

Thirst.
To fly, to die,
Surrendering all name.
To simply
Be
What Is,
Night,
Flame,
Same.

A moment with God,
Forgetful one,
Transforms all.
Bathe in the
Infinity
That surrounds
And fills
Without exception,
Even this, the
Thought
Now in your mind.
Exist in peace.
All
Is kind.

Day
Once again, arises, sings,
Filled with millions
Of miraculous things.
Heaven on Earth
Here everywhere lies,
As always,
In the beholder's eyes.

Each creature, leaf,
Pebble, atom, every
Form
Glides a path
Of function
In deep Divine norm.
A human finds purpose,
Heart lighting the way.
Life
Becomes Being,
Too simple
To say.

Hafiz,
You touch me
Through distances strange
Of language, culture, miles,
And vast many years.
You make me laugh,
And wipe my tears,
Just as you said you would,
If I would lend you my ears.
Grand gentleman of God,
Your love poured into words,
I sit with you here now,
So drunk, and sing with you
In God's sweet flock of birds.

Scientists have been studying
This swirling array of sparks
We call home.
And among the minutia
Of the micro-movements
Of all that galactic light,
They look for
Others like us.

But we are too dim and weak
In our being,
In our seeing
To be detected.
It seems
A greater beingness,
A greater seeingness
Is required
For us to
Find ourselves.

I am a tree,
Leaves rustling
In Your wind.

That, that
Is, is.

Starry sparks shower,
Fire swirls, scientists say.
Bursting points, bright,
Arc in curls,
Rosette together,
Scatter, as the
Velvet dark night
Deep with distance,
Steadfast,
Deep with mystery,
Makes a perfect
Softly dark display
In which to show forth scintillant
Cascades
In all their perfect
Stately, falling, ever all
Proliferant
Array.

Let us
Enjoy this swiftly fleeting
Moment
Of this brief
Galactic day.

There before us,
All of us,
All the time,
Whether one stops to wonder,
Or does not,
There is the
Infinite One.
So complex.
So simple.
So obvious.
So mysterious.
All the forms at once.
No form at all.
Aloof, not
Caring for persons.
Loving.
For He holds
Every aspect of skin
That you have,

So delicately,
That you live.
Uncountable worlds
Do their daily business
All around us
In the deep surrounding skies
Of every size
Before our eyes,
Yet we see but
A night's bright dotted
Wallpaper
And a life
Of signs
And sighs.

Broken off, is this small
Fragment here, this tiny grain
Of You,
That sees, knows
But little,
Loves
Only meanly,
Has only
Fitful dreams
About what's Real.
But when I ask,
And hold out my little
Jigsaw puzzle arms,
You slide me into place
In You,
And more of the
Big picture of all
Knowing and of Love
Instantly appears.

All the missingness
At these edges
Disappears, and
All the puzzle world is me,
And, too,
The table where it rests.
Fragment gone,
There are
No more fears,
No tests.

Then comes
Some Formless
Thumb that
Strikes the feelings
Of my heart
Like strings to strum.
My inner voices
All go dumb.
And Silence takes my hand
And holds the pencil
To the page
And writes
Some words in this
The language of the age
A ripple
In the seas of time
A sound
A simple line.

You have robbed me,
Dear One, of my
Serious side.
Shouldn't I be more
Worried
About retirement?
You are making me
The grasshopper
Instead of the ant.
I spend all my time fiddling with You.
Shouldn't I be
A little worried
That I'm not worried?
Somehow,
I keep putting all
The eggs in
Your basket
Again.

All the dancing seconds
Join hands and, laughing,
Merge,
The minutes, days, and hours,
Already long gone,
Dissolved.
Micro, nano, gone,
With eon, year, millennium, age.
Continuum, One,
Hello.
How cleverly you
Hid among us,
In disguise,
Before
Our very eyes.

We are so hungry.
We take One
Fresh Life,
Dice it up,
Sized to taste,
Apply our sauce,
Flavored,
As only we prefer,
And, only then,
Dine,
Civilized,
Frail.
We are not like
The wild ones
Upon the icy mountains
Who can merge with
Life
With one
Inhale.

Sidelit castle clouds
Ride the silver sky
At morn.
Another
Brilliant day
Is born.
Leaves lightly
Touch,
Brush the surface
Of the air.
The birds, puffed,
Ponder silence,
Sitting there.
Dew diamonds hang
Everywhere.
Sudden gold strings
Strike through.
Busy noises rise
Under blue skies
All new.

We sort through
All these things
To find the good, for us.
Sorting and rummaging
We go,
Looking for a prized
Moment.
Well:

Here it is.

Feel how it glows, so
Magnificently
Alive.

Nothing that you see,
Touch or think,
Here,
Is not amazing,
When your heart
Is like This.

The bonds of love
Are there,
Everywhere.
They, soft,
Hand in hand,
The lovers hold,
And hard, when
Shoulder to shoulder,
The embattled soldiers, bold, Stand.
In winding traffic ribbons,
Love moves through,
Swift, smooth.
In the logic
Of the bond of society, star,
Atom, cell wall,
Love weaves the
Intricate basketry
Of All.

By some
Strange series of accidents
I have arrived
Here:
This name, these friends,
This job, this wife.
I did not seem to plan
This life.
Yet here I am,
One tiny fragment of
White sugar in Your bowl,
Among a billion others
Different, but the same,
And ready to dissolve today
Upon Your tongue
Should Your
Great spoon
Arrive this way.

Your Wind comes
And blows away
The few straws
I have collected,
And catches, too,
The last one
I am
Clutching.
And I, too, am
Blown away,
Only Wind.

I rest
My case.

Dear Truth
Of Oneness,
You have
So many enemies here.
People wrap themselves
Against You
As if your breeze
Were an artic gale.
They will turn
Their barrage of grudges
Against even You
To defend their outposts.
Sometimes it seems
That Your friends
Are few
And far between.

Especially when I tumble
And desert You myself,

Failing to forgive, see
Love.

Yet there You are
Always
Everywhere
In the softest of
Patience.

Foolish
Gossamer
On wind
Imagining
It is
Piloting.
Foolish
Antenna
Receiving,
Imagining
It is
Broadcasting,
Scripting.
Foolish paper,
Imagining
It is speaking
The words
Occurring
Upon it.

Foolish Man,
Imagining
The genes,
The thoughts,
The words,
The actions,
The selfness felt,
The purse of
Treasure,
To be
Alone,
Unique.

Happinesses
Vary
Very much.
Some are
Shouted in the beer.
Some enraptured
In a velvet touch.
Some are found
In tiny giggles,
Innocent, and
Loved so much.
Some are found
In crowds, all
Loud and
Powered up.
Some are found
In active thrill
Of deftest skill.
Some, even,
In a kill.

Some are found
In subtle
Sight and sound
At dawn.
One
Is found
When all the rest
Are gone.

Before these houses,
Poles, wires, cars,
There were only
Hills, wind, chaparral,
And sea.
These are all
Still here to see.
Man's items
Come and go.
Ever, quietly,
Winds blow.

All the lines
Have collapsed
Having no directions
For having now
No ends or beginnings,
The melting segments left
Glittering in the sun,
Dust flecks floating
Deep in the air.

Yesterday
My mind
Was there.

Tick
Tock,
Turn,
Rock.
Stones of time
Surround,
Swirl,
All event,
One
Boulder
Burl.
All
Change,
No
Change,
However
Hot
Fire
Burn,

However
Hot
Seeking
Learn.

Morning.
The world rises, fills
With movements, things
Coming and going.
Man fills with urges
To move, make, gain,
Stop pain.

There is sun,
Wind, rain.

Please,
Flood
My rivers.
Break
My banks.
Deepen
Me.
Let this
Secret love,
Disguised
As ordinary things
Out.
Let this
Gentle happiness
Tenderly
Shout.

As age rises
Into higher numbers
And ending looms,
It is not,
Somewhere ahead,
A growing sense of
Shortness
That I feel, but sweet
Infinitude,
Blowing in
The open door
There, before
My face,
A soft cradling
Of
Grace.

Love is a
Decision.
Opening the heart
To husband, wife,
To fellow man,
To God,
Is done the same as
Opening the hand.
The search for love ends
When we discover
Our heart strings,
Like those of a purse
With no bottom.
We may pull open,
Wide,
At any time.
Take,
Disburse.

The salt doll
Dissolves
Into the sea,
As Sri Ramakrishna,
Seeing,
Being Sea,
So sweetly sang,
His body dancing
Like a sparkling wave.
The waves of ecstasy
Emerge among
The body forms of men
And shine, in glancing, sparkling
Sun Divine.
The scene recounted
For a hundred years,
The story sung,
Intoxicating
Vintage wine.

Sometimes
My footstep stops
Upon an edge,
A precipice, where
Nothing forward is,
No place to step,
Except perhaps,
Some air.
And, pausing there,
Inhaling
All,
Some land appears.
Another step I take,
Moving on
Without a fall.

Collectively
We course
Within the veins
Of this old world
In dreams, desires, fears,
Each person
Moving through their years,
Moving, coursing
In a pulse as one.
One beating heart
Impels us on our way
As each, in traffic,
Does their part
To breathe and feed
And nourish
Life
Today.

Like clear water
Emerging in a place of
Dampened ground,
This moment overflows.
Clarity moistens this
Crevasse in time.
One sip brings
Cool contentment
Of a loving union with
What Is.
What started as a bubbling
Curiosity to know
Began to flow
Acceptance,
Soft enough to touch the
Perfect
That is moving in all forms.
Thirst gone, listening,
I muse and watch the
Glistening
Emerge and go.

Love waits
And holds the moment
For another,
Like a coat
To slip into.

A bit of
Gratitude
Cures
Fear.

This moment,
A cave
In the mountains
Of time,
Pauses quiet,
Deep in the
Intergalactic sky.
I sit here,
Relaxed,
All
Only
I.

A wandering one
Returns.
And I am only self,
Or selfness.
And attention, having scattered,
Gathers,
As the birds in autumn
Gather a great presence.
And this person, like
Flock in formation,
Is but a collection of
Generic and eternal parts
In flight together
In the Sky
Infinite.
Moving on,
I rest
Within the quiet glories
Of the
Day.

I would not be able to make
So wondrous a thing
As a fingernail
Or a hair.
So much the less,
An eye, a heart.
So I am not sure that
It is I
Who move this finger.

This ephemeral wraith
Called 'I,'
That inhabits this
Miraculous Being
Can only barely try
To take credit
For anything
In the midst of this
Grandeur.

Let
Fleeting form fly.
Do not cling.
Be One with That
That uses form
To sing.

And should a sense of
Personal responsibility
Arise,

Relax.
Be wise.

Allow it to disperse
Into the skies above,
And feel instead
The Love
That holds and nurtures
All.
And act instead
In states of
Effortless surprise,
Harmonious,
Wide.

Your heart can cease
Its nervous cries,

Its tries to
Steer the wind and tide.

Relax.
Be only
All
Without
Disguise.

Morning.
Clouds disperse, and
The Earth is crystal clear.
The mares of the night
Whereon mind was riding
Have fled
Into the shadowed meadows.

Brightness rules,
With the precious firmness
Of Reality,
That holds us
So delicately
On Its finger.

Newness
Bursts forth
Unexpected surprises,

As unique combinations
Of the eternally old
Are formed
With utter
Continuousness.
Life's proud preciousness
Marches,
Filled
With loving wealth.

Beauty shines
Everywhere.
Cover your body
With mouths
To drink.
Skin, eye, ear,
Tongue, nose,
All the inner senses,
The antennae of
The bones,
The lightening sensor
Of the brain,
Let them open wide,
All, and flood together,
One nerve tree
Shaking in the
Holy Wind
With all the leaves
Alive,

One eye of
Sensate skin.

Let
All
In.

Bubble shell,
Infinitely thin,
Do you not hold
All without,
All within?

Love
Finds its start
At center
Of a bursting heart.
Do not wait
For time or tide
To bring you Love.
You will find
The spring
Of awesome flood
Inside.

Questions
Chasing answers
Dart around
Eroding walls.

Oh.
Did you feel that?
There is Breath
In the clay.

The waves that
Meet the Shore
Forever break,
Roar,
And fall into
A million tears,
Then join into a
Fluid rush
Back into the
Surging sea,
The Ocean,
Once again,
To
Be.

Morning News:
This
The breaking headline is:
There is nothing, really,
Ever new.
That, that matters
Is
Always
Ever
True.

We are here
Condensed
Like morning dew
From light of stars,
To be as mist, and fluid,
And as stone,
To be as leaf, as blossom,
And as wood,
To be as creature
Sensitive of skin, eye, ear,
To hunt for food and mate,
And kill the objects
Of our hate,
And love the good.
Yet always, it is true
Even on this globe that turn
With Mars, Jupiter, Saturn,
That we are more than
Animal alone.

We are the
Light Eternal
That has always shone.
As this perspective
We can see,
We can
Be
Absolutely
Free.

Human beings,
I have just been sitting here
With Hafiz
Remembering and
Laughing, and
Pouring a deep draught of
Sweet Night Sky
Sparkling
Into our old Earth's
Beautiful, waiting
Dry cup.
So, Yes! All,
Please enjoy.
Let your hearts
Overflow
One into another.
Suddenly notice great beauty.
Like a little girl or boy,
Feel yourself carried along

In the long sweet day
Of a beloved child
At play.
In the depths of this pouring
There is no stopping.
Feel free
To join this company
Of drowned
Laughing ones
Lying, mouths open,
Flat out on Tavern floor,
Accepting from the
Tavern Keeper,
More, more,
More.

A
Hurrying man,
Dropping all
Concern and plan,
Becomes
All-quiet Sky.

Resting in
Soft delight,
Such Man
Is
Only
Night.

For me,
No poem
Is worth the small
Black dye
That it may occupy,
That does not
Open
Poor contracted
Mind, heart, eye
To see, to
Be
Some softly open
Sky.

ABOUT THE AUTHOR

Who is this Author?

This question is best answered by looking into the author's finished pages, which stand ready for the reading.

But, in the interests of social convention, here is some biographical data to clothe this character.

The early years of the author were steeped in several cultures.

The author as a youngster spent long hours and years in the laconic hard scrabble labor of rural Appalachian mountain life, his father's roots.

The author's mother came from the prosperous flatter farmlands of rural Maryland, close-knit family people of an old Pennsylvania Dutch background, who sang sweet acapela harmonies, while praying and working together.

The author grew up in both influences, while living in the midst of the robust cultural mix of the Washington D.C. environs.

The author left high school blessed with a scholarship to an exceptionally fine university, where he spent his four years, wandering somewhat, among the peaks of Man's intellectual achievement.

The Writing Seminars were among the most memorable experiences of the time there, hours of sharing words among fellow poets, lounging around a large and darkly aged conference table.

In the cultural uproar of the 1968-69 senior year, studies were eclipsed, as the author's interests exploded into off-campus venues and activities, not in the political actions of the day, but in the spiritual, metaphysical and transcendental.

In this vibrant time, the City of Baltimore burgeoned with opportunities for close friendships, learning and practice with various yogis from India, gypsies, highly conscious artists and mystics of various kinds, along with a matured Theosophical Lodge and Rosicrucian Lodge, AMORC, all of this guided by the posters and amazingly well-stocked shelves of the New Age Bookstore, where meditators gathered, crowded together seated on the floor on Tuesday evenings. The author was a part of spiritual communes that started up and renovated spaces in which to work and live together.

This storm of Baltimore life came on, seemed to last forever, and then passed suddenly, with an abrupt departure to a place in Vermont's north woods.

Then stretched decades of living various places, supported by working with hands and small building business activity, with years of life's lessons in family living with children, years of a spiritual-martial practice, years spent close with a guru from India, and years of working with a spiritually oriented mind training course.

In recent years, the art of word-craft, practiced since childhood, came to the fore.

A body of privately written work slowly accumulated, waiting for the writer to feel ready for its release.

FROM THE PUBLISHER

Hello Dear Reader!

We hope that you are enjoying *Falling Into All* as much as we enjoyed producing it and putting it out into the world.

We also hope that you feel it worthwhile to help spread the word about this book in your community of like-minded readers.

Your review on Amazon will go a long way toward letting other people know about *Falling Into All*.

If you would like to help out (every little bit helps), will you please post a review on Amazon, or where you purchased a copy?

Do you know someone who would enjoy reading *Forever Free?* Download a free copy on our website, at WiseWordWind.com

Plus, we offer weekly fresh words from Ben by email and on social media. Be sure to subscribe and join our audience of loyal readers.

If you want to connect with Ben directly, email him:at Ben@WiseWordWind.com.

Thank you!

~The Team at Wise Word Wind Press

CPSIA information can be obtained
at www.ICGtesting.com
Printed in the USA
BVHW052038021122
650798BV00002B/13